ROCKY MOUNTAIN NEWS

With the sun just breaking over the Montana prairie, this cowboy's day is already hours old. Despite the long hours, low wages and hard work, most cowboys wouldn't trade places with anyone on Earth. Being out there on a horse in the dawn light, seeing all that big country and being a part of it all, life's as good as it gets.

ISBN: 1-884850-02-2

LIBRARY OF CONGRESS CATALOG CARD NUMBER: 96-67578

*E*nveloped in a cloud of dust and smoke, a young cowhand struggles to keep his hold on a kicking, bawling calf as its hide is seared with a brand on a ranch near Lame Deer, Montana. Branding is a western tradition that keeps rustlers at bay and helps owners identify their cattle when they're mixed with other herds on the open range.

KRAKEL'S WEST

Photographs and Text by
DEAN KRAKEL

Edited & Designed by
J. BRUCE BAUMANN

PRIMARILY, I'M A ROAD SHOOTER

The best times are the quiet ones

I never intended to become a photographer. I wanted to be a cowboy. Part of that dream was fulfilled while working on ranches in Montana and Colorado. For a time, I even fancied myself a rodeo hand. But there were inherent problems with the cowboy career choice. Although I loved the way of life, horses make me nervous, and I don't have the patience to work cattle. Nor could I ever overcome the nauseating fear that gripped me every time I sat down on a saddle bronc and nodded for the chute gate to open.

Sometimes finding out what you aren't cut out for in life takes a long time. It's expensive and painful. But if it hadn't been for horses and cows and rodeo, I might not have discovered photography.

I bought my first camera when I was sixteen and working for the Stirrup Bar Ranch at a cow camp on Colorado's Black Mesa. A way of life was disappearing, and I wanted to hold on to it with something more tangible than memories. The way a photograph stopped time seemed magical.

A Canadian bronc rider who took rodeo action pictures and sold them to other contestants introduced me to the mysteries of the darkroom. I was instantly hooked. Taking pictures was fun. Then I discovered that people would pay me to take them.

There's hardly any way to disguise a satellite dish, especially in the woods near Essex, Montana. But you can try to blend it in with the surroundings. With a touch of whimsy, this television junkie pays homage to the West while plugging in to the 21st century.

*T*he wild animals that roam the West often are no match for man's encroachment. Pronghorn antelope and barbed wire don't mix well (above). Unlike other hooved and horned prairie natives, these speedsters won't jump a fence, preferring to slip under the wire. But the technique sometimes leads to a fatal entanglement. Hanging from a tree in Colorado's White River National Forest, a dead deer, covered by an insect-proof bag, awaits the skinning knife (right). There is nothing subtle about the killing during autumn's hunting season. Hunters are the economic lifeblood of many small towns, infusing local economies with cash that will sustain them through the long winter ahead.

During the past seven years as a staff photographer for Denver's *Rocky Mountain News*, I've been fortunate. Many of my assignments let me do what I like to do best — travel the West.

Although the city generates plenty of exciting news stories that must be covered, my most cherished assignments are the ones that take me out of town, away from the grit of city life for a few hours, a day or a week. I may wake up in Denver, but I may go to sleep in Durango, Moab, Deadwood, Bozeman or Cheyenne.

The downside, of course, is that newspaper photographers usually don't have the luxury of time. Arrivals and departures are quick. We see things once and move on. Our job is to show what's happening now, to make a deadline, to fill a space and to do it again tomorrow and the next day and the day after that.

Primarily, I'm a road shooter. Meaning, I guess, that I take most of my pictures by the side of a road. Sometimes there are rivers to be floated and trails to be walked or skied, sunrises and sunsets and beautiful vistas to savor with no immediate deadlines hovering overhead. Sometimes there are family and friends and colleagues for company, but mostly it's just me, hurrying between assignments.

The best times are the quiet ones, when I'm alone with my thoughts, speeding across an empty space on an empty highway with the big view all around, the windows rolled down and the scent of pine and sage and the cold bite of mountain air pouring in and nothing to do but look for pictures.

I'm always discovering something new. No matter how many times I've driven a road or passed through a town, there's always something new to see.

For the most part, then, these are found images, places and people and scenes along the way, the result of a lifelong love affair with the highways and byways of the West.

— *DEAN KRAKEL*

T he West is the domain of cowboys and their horses, and dawn is the daily moment of reckoning. A cowboy on the Padlock Ranch in Montana targets his morning mount with a lariat (above). Preparing for the day's work on the Chaparrosa Ranch in southwest Texas, vaqueros move their horses toward the corral (above right). On the Chaparrosa, vaqueros don't rope their mounts. In a time-honored tradition known as the formando, the horses have been taught to line up when they hear the crack of a buggy whip and a command from the cowboss. The vaqueros then walk forward and bridle their mounts.

*D*ressed against the chill of a Montana summer morning, cowboys on the Padlock Ranch stand ready to begin a long day's work. On the ranch, which sprawls across a half-million acres of northern Wyoming and southern Montana, scenes reminiscent of ranching a century ago are still commonplace. One such constant is the chuck wagon (below). Although the wagons are pulled these days by pickups, not teams of horses, cowboys still gather in the cook tent to drink coffee, roll cigarettes and eat breakfast in the predawn.

Gloriously golden at autumn's peak, a cottonwood grove hugs the Yellowstone River in central Montana. Truly, the cottonwood is the tree of the West. Wherever it grows, there is cool shade and water. Its gnarled form soothes the eye after a long day on the barren high plains. Its branches offer shelter and songbirds, the promise of a campfire. Wind rustling among its leaves, the cottonwood lifts the heart.

R obert Nichols is a poet, a gentle bear of a man with a windblown white beard, Zen mind and a nose flattened in a bar-room brawl. He lives in a tepee on Guanella Pass near Grant, Colorado. Once, he had a regular house, a regular job and a regular life, but he gave them up to pursue his dream of living in the mountains and writing full time. "I felt that to be true to my art, I would have to give up any semblance of what normal life should be," he says. "I'm not here to prove anything. I'm not a mountain man. This is what poets can afford." But life in a tepee during the long mountain winters can give even a poet too much solitude. "There's something about a banjo that just makes you laugh," he says. "A banjo's the best thing for chasing loneliness away."

Dan Muldoon (left) grew up in New York but left city life to become a cowboy in Colorado. He works for the Magness Land & Cattle Company in South Park and lives in a cow camp several miles from the small town of Jefferson. "This country has all the parts that it needs," he says. "Wild country and as much humanity as a person needs to have. I guess I have different priorities than the rest of the world."

Eppie Archuleta's richly colored hand-woven rugs have won her fame. In 1985, she was awarded a National Heritage Fellowship, the nation's highest award for achievement in traditional arts. Born into a family of fourth-generation weavers — her mother was still producing rugs at the age of 93 — Archuleta began weaving when she was 8. In the 1940s, she moved with her husband, Frank (in background), to Alamosa, Colorado, in the San Luis Valley. "My weaving has always made money, but not as good as now," she says, expressing surprise that collectors pay as much as $1,200 for one of her rugs. "They have always had value to me. Now they have value to others."

*S*ome mornings it doesn't pay to be a cowboy. A cold rain at dawn means bad things — a wet horse, wet saddle, wet cattle and water pouring off your hat brim. In a cow camp in the Bighorn Mountains of Wyoming, Arnie Cooper lingers at the kitchen table, hoping that maybe, just maybe, the storm will pass.

*W*estern ropers have two styles, tie hard and fast or dally. With tie hard and fast, the rope is tied to the saddle horn. Dally ropers wrap their rope around the horn, a deft maneuver when there's a bucking hunk of livestock on the rope's other end. Corvin Cooper is a classic dally man, dragging another calf to the branding fire.

I was hanging out behind the chutes at a rodeo in Montana when this fellow stopped in front of me. He'd been celebrating, that was certain. I never learned his name or what he did or where he was from. "Take my picture," he said. And I did.

T he Pendleton Roundup in Pendleton, Oregon, is one of the most colorful rodeos in America, a wild and woolly western event that takes place in the fall, long after most tourists have gone home. It's a rodeo for the hard core and a huge gathering for Native Americans. Compressed by a long lens, this tepee village isn't as crowded as it looks. The tepees aren't just for show. People live in them, like this woman, stirring long before her neighbors.

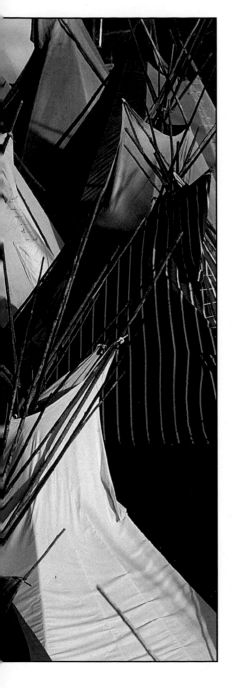

ool in summer, warm in winter and the ulti-
mate in quick take-down, put-up portability,
the plains Indian tepee was perhaps the
most perfect dwelling ever devised for life on
the high plains. This concrete tepee in
Browning, Montana, is another matter. Warm in
summer, cool in winter and not at all easy to
move, the tepee once was a cafe serving
tourists on their way to Glacier National Park.
Now, it's somebody's house.

W hen Andy Howe bought property along Colorado 112 near Del Norte, this antler tree came with it. The tree consists of elk and deer antlers, crowned by a plastic deer head. Howe doesn't know how the tree came into being, just that the former owner was a junk collector of sorts. He's had many offers to sell it but has refused them all. "I'd rather just keep the tree for me," he says.

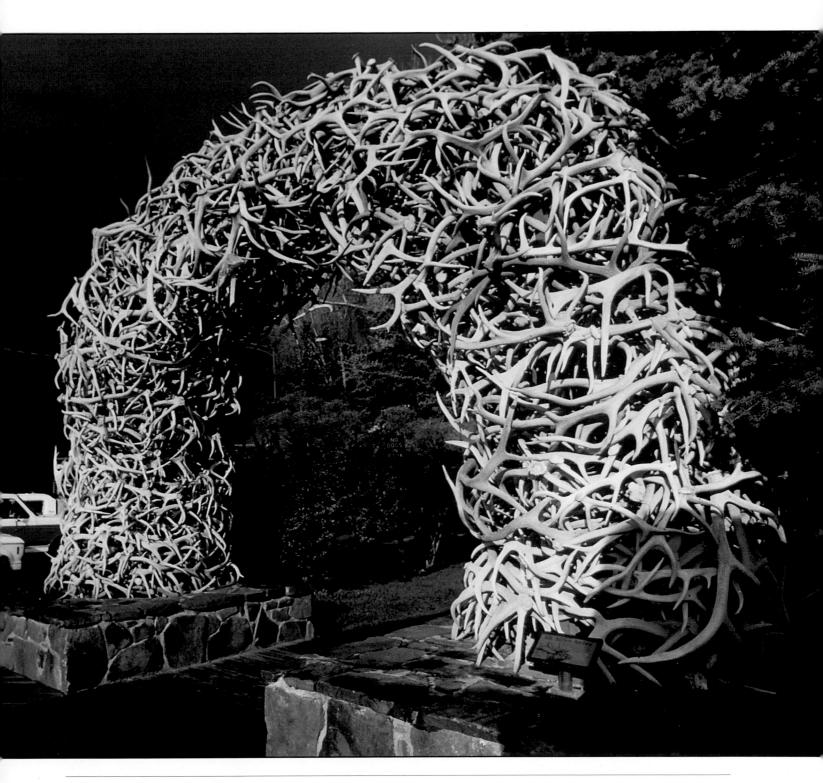

Every spring, bull elk, deer and moose shed their antlers. If left to nature, the antlers deteriorate and return nutrients to the soil. But humans prize antlers for decoration and the manufacture of all sorts of knick-knacks. In Asia, powdered elk antler is used as an aphrodisiac. Many western towns sport elk horn arches, but few are as massive as the ones that grace each corner of Pioneer Park in Jackson, Wyoming.

A full moon sets over the Sangre de Cristo Mountains of southern Colorado, but it's a quarter moon that marks the boys' outhouse at the century-old Willow Creek School in the Wet Mountain Valley. Although the one-room school hasn't seen students in decades, the outhouse is still functional and a welcome sight for travelers in this rural area.

Pinedale, Wyoming, artists Pip and Duane Brandt belong to a group called Kunstwaffen, German for "art weapons." Among the Brandts' weapons is their horse Quasar. When President George Bush went fishing in the Brandts' neck of the woods, Pip painted the horse with the message "Listen to me." The Brandts once painted poetry on an entire herd of cattle. "We have plastic and wood and metal things with writing all over them in our culture," reasons Duane Brandt. "Why not write on animals?"

Mike Turner made these giant arrows from telephone poles and placed them beside his store, the Hogan Trading Post, along U.S. 160 near Mancos, Colorado. The arrows are replicas of giant arrows his father built at a store on old U.S. 66 near Albuquerque, New Mexico. The Hogan is a thirty-year-old landmark that sells jewelry, antique saddles, spurs and bits.

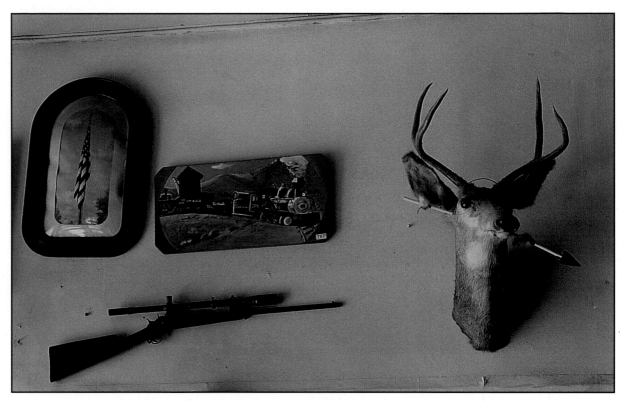

Walls in rural gas stations quite often are works of art. Every bit of space is covered with antiques and memorabilia — anything that catches the owner's fancy or satisfies a whim. Wall art often is a collective effort put together through the years by successions of owners and customers. The owner of this wall is Chuck Glaze of the QT Store in Parlin, Colorado.

*T*he West is a land of relics from the human experience in a vast landscape. A bullet-riddled car (above) lies along the Kokopelli Trail, which winds for 128 miles through the desert from Loma, Colorado, to Moab, Utah. Once an ancient migration route for early Native Americans, the trail takes its name from a humpbacked, flute-playing mythical being popular in Anasazi culture. Cisco, Utah, is home to the White Buffalo Disco (right). Located in the desert between the towns of Moab, Utah, and Grand Junction, Colorado, the White Buffalo was converted from a gas station to a club in hopes of attracting patrons from both towns. But Cisco wasn't ready for a disco, and the White Buffalo died.

D ew bejewels frosted meadow grasses as an elk herd greets a misty dawn along the Gibbon River in Yellowstone National Park. Established in 1872, the park is home to one of the largest concentrations of elk in North America.

J ackalopes are a cross between jackrabbits and antelopes and exist in only a few places in the West. It is said that the mythical animal is visible only during lightning flashes and generally only then by citizens who are returning home from their favorite saloon. Douglas, Wyoming, has the distinction of being the jackalope capital of the world, a title it claims with pride. This concrete tribute to the beast stood for many years on the Douglas County Fairgrounds. Now it adds flavor to a park near the center of town.

*I*n the language of the Crow Indians, the word *absaro-ka* means children of the large beaked bird. It was the name they used for themselves. Today, the word is the name of a mountain range in Montana containing some of the most ruggedly beautiful country in North America. When the land is summer green and damp from an afternoon thundershower, it is easy to sense the mystery and spirit of those early people, to know why they called this country along the Yellowstone River home.

Poetry in slow motion, horses gallop down a highway near Miles City, Montana, on their way from the stockyards to the pasture where they'll spend the night.

T he horse knows he's caught, and the game of roper and roped is over for one cowboy on the Padlock Ranch in Montana. Roping is the most efficient way for a dozen cowboys to quickly catch their mounts. Although the sly horses try to avoid being caught, once the loop slides over their heads, they rarely struggle.

F resh off the prairie, wild horses await their fate in a Miles City, Montana, corral. Thousands of wild horses roamed the Montana plains at the turn of the century, cut loose by homesteaders who abandoned their claims. Only a few wild horses remain today. Ranchers call them broomtails because their ungroomed tails often brush the ground.

The dawn sun streaming beneath its legs, a horse on the Padlock Ranch in Montana throws its head to avoid a cowboy's loop and the call to work. At the beginning of a roundup, a cowboy is assigned a string of horses. Horses are sometimes changed twice a day, depending on the workload. Some horses are specialists, used for roping or sorting cattle. Some are great travelers; others have good cow sense. Some are fast, some are slow, some lazy, some calm, some high-strung. Not only is a cowboy roping his day's mount, he's roping his working partner.

Bucking horses come in all shapes, sizes and colors, like these horses squeezed into a corral at the Miles City Bucking Horse Auction in Miles City, Montana. At the auction, a tradition every spring since 1950, horses are bought, sold and traded based on their ability to throw off a rider.

*L*aughter and muted conversation, the nickering of horses, the occasional jingle of a spur and creak of saddle leather — these are the sounds of daybreak as riders begin work on the Padlock Ranch in Montana.

*C*overed with dust, manure, blood and sweat, a cowboy strains to hold the leg of a calf as it is struck with a hot iron and branded. Branding crews work in teams. One cowboy holds the calf's hind legs, another sits on the head. Each calf, some weighing close to a hundred pounds, must be thrown to the ground, one after the other, all day long.

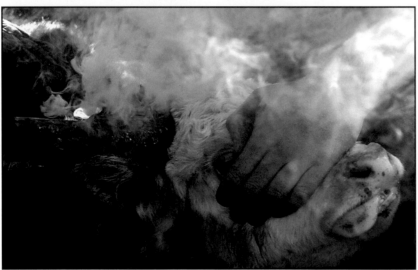

*S*moke, the smell of burning hair and a calf's frightened bawl fill the air during branding. Calves wear the brand for life. During branding, calves also are dehorned, castrated, vaccinated and sometimes earmarked and dewlapped. A skilled branding crew can complete the task in under a minute.

C orvin Cooper sorts through a corral full of cattle on the Padlock Ranch in Montana, swinging his rope gently back and forth as he looks for a calf to rope. Calves are roped by the heels and dragged to the branding fire. To watch an expert roper working atop his best horse is to watch an artist at work.

Rodeo is the hard edge of western life put out for public view. The sport has evolved a long way from its origins in everyday tasks done on the range. Today's rodeo cowboy and cowgirl are professional athletes like their counterparts in the ball-playing sports. But rodeo is a hard life, much of it spent going down the road. There are no coaches, corporate sponsors, agents or management teams. Contestants pay for the privilege of competing — and the chance to be bucked off, kicked, horned, stomped or otherwise maimed. Critics say rodeo is cruel to the animals. It is a hard sport but not a cruel one, and it is hardest of all on the human participants.

Elephant Hill in the Needles District of Canyonlands National Park, Utah, is aptly named because it's such a beastly big thing to get over. The trail climbs over slickrock and rubble, then plunges down a series of steep switchbacks. But from the top, the view of the park's needlelike formations is worth the effort, especially in the quiet of a canyon country dawn.

F or many years, this hulk-
ing buffalo skull created
by artist Vic Lemmon
guarded the entrance of the
Grubb n' Tubb cafe and
laundromat in Dubois,
Wyoming. Grubb n' Tubb
patrons could wash their
clothes and eat at the same
time. Today, the cafe is just
a bit of local history, and
the skull dominates the
doorway of a veterinary
clinic.

An unspoken code of the West is that all road signs must be shot full of holes. This one's near the eastern Colorado town of Kiowa. Who in the world shoots signs? When do they do it? Is it a spur-of-the-moment thing? Does it signify a deep dislike of authority?

Here's one rule of the rural roadway: Mailboxes are bound to be shot at by trigger-happy passers-by. Most mailbox owners, however, don't encourage the practice. This mailbox (left) along Colorado 109 south of La Junta is an exception. It's made of steel and is impervious to assault.

*S*and dunes dwarf a small cluster of cottonwood trees caught in evening light at the Great Sand Dunes National Monument in southern Colorado. Dramatic patterns of light, shadow and form attracted visitors long before the monument was established in 1932. The dunes, deposited when sand-laden winds slammed into the adjacent Sangre de Cristo Mountains, cover 89 square miles and rise more than 750 feet.

B eauty is always around the next bend in Crested Butte, Colorado. During the summer, the lush meadows beneath the West Elk Mountains bloom in kaleidoscopic profusion, filling the air with an intoxicating perfume. Early one summer morning, I found photographer Nathan Bilow shooting two models in a field of flowers. When the sun went behind a cloud, Nathan took a break, and one of the models walked off by herself, momentarily alone in the splendor.

E mma Fuller looks out upon her home through the frosted window of a jeep in Yellowstone Park. Emma's father, Steven Fuller, has been the winter caretaker at Canyon Village since 1973. When I visited them, the Fullers were living in a century-old house on a hillside above the Yellowstone River's Grand Canyon. Bison grazed in the yard and pine martins squabbled beneath the kitchen floor. An occasional grizzly bear left paw prints on the front door. During the winters, it took a 40-mile snowmobile trip to reach the nearest town.

Bill Dexter spent most of his life trapping in the Montana mountains near the Cinnabar Basin. He hauled his water from a nearby creek, walked everywhere he went and kept a year's supply of beans, flour and coffee inside his house in fifty-gallon drums. He boasted he hadn't shaved in sixty years.

With freshly gathered eggs in each hand, Henry Salazar, 75, poses next to a trophy from the elk-hunting season. Salazar, who owns a ranch near Manassa, Colorado, in the San Luis Valley, traces his family's roots to Spaniards who settled in the valley in the early 1800s. Spanish explorers first entered the valley in the 1600s.

F or a hundred miles, the White Rim Trail in southern Utah winds through a dramatic high-desert landscape above the Colorado and Green rivers. Windswept, sun-baked and desolate, the trail climbs to its most lonesome point on the Murphy Hogback, deep in the Island of the Sky District of Canyonlands National Park.

*E*ighty-five-year-old Lawrence Storm (left) of Cañon City, Colorado, has been fiddling around since he was a child. In his younger days, he used to ride a horse twenty miles to a dance, play the fiddle all night and ride home at dawn. He's made some fiddles, repaired some fiddles, bought, sold, traded and collected fiddles. He still plays during Sunday afternoon get-togethers with family and friends. But now, he laments, he forgets a tune "before I can play it."

*J*ackson, Wyoming, attorney Gerry Spence has represented the plain and prominent for thirty years. A charismatic crusader to some, a self promoter to others, Spence successfully defended Imelda Marcos and won a multimillion-dollar judgment for the estate of anti-nuclear activist Karen Silkwood. An accomplished author and photographer, Spence believes he has only just begun to reach the height of his powers.

My friend Connie Schwiering spent a lifetime painting the Teton Mountains of Wyoming. From his home on Antelope Flats, a view of the peaks filled the living room windows. Connie painted every day, outdoors on location in the summer and in his studio during the winter. He never tired of his subject. He told me it was the mountains' ever-changing moods that so captivated him. I took this photograph while returning from a visit to Connie's grave. He and his wife, Mary Ethel, are buried in an aspen grove among wildflowers within sight of the mountains they loved.

W inding past cottonwood trees flecked with autumn's gold, the Yellowstone River spills across the Montana plains on its way toward joining the Missouri River in North Dakota. From its source in the Absaroka Mountains of north-western Wyoming, the river travels 671 miles through Yellowstone National Park and across Montana. Untamed by any dam, the Yellowstone is the longest free-flow-ing river left in the continental United States. By the time it reaches eastern Montana, it is near-ly a mile wide.

plentiful corn harvest finds Bartlett and Company's grain elevators stuffed to capacity in Yuma, Colorado. Jim Swopes is dwarfed by more than 400,000 bushels of corn being piled on the ground outside until additional storage space can be found.

Racing an approaching storm, a combine harvests wheat on the John Stillman farm near Faith, South Dakota. Wheat farmers spend nearly all their time watching the sky, hoping for rain during the growing season and praying for no rain during the harvest. A fast-moving storm can batter a field with hail or set it afire with a lightning strike. Combine crews follow the wheat harvest from Texas to Canada, working late into the night.

At the head of Marston Creek beneath Wall Mountain, horse packer Jack Swenson leads his packstring across a high meadow in the Absaroka Mountains of northwestern Wyoming. Protected by the rugged terrain, Marston Creek receives few human visitors, and most of those, like Swenson, are merely passing through.

Young boys still want to be cow-boys, aspiring to riding and roping and a life in the open. Some are lucky enough to find a place that welcomes them. I don't know this boy's name, but he was mighty proud to be working on a roundup crew for the Padlock Ranch in Montana — and mighty serious about his responsibilities. Every morning before sunup, he wrangled the horses and drove them into camp before the cowboys finished their breakfast.

Another hard day's work behind them, cowboys head for home in central Montana. I don't know how long scenes like this will last. Cows are controversial these days. Some people want them kicked off federal land. Others blame them for global warming and heart disease. But I hope there are always cattle in the West and riders on horseback in the long grass beside them.

*W*esterners have always been fashion leaders. Just look at how cowboy hats, blue jeans and pointed-toe boots caught on with the rest of the world. Bleached steer skulls that languished in the back forty for years now adorn city-slicker apartments as wall hangings. Who knows, maybe belts made of empty snuff cans will catch on someday. For now, though, this belt is one of a kind, made and worn with pride in Como, Colorado.

*U*nder a darkening sky, cowboys on the Padlock Ranch in Montana ready themselves for another day's work during the spring roundup. From Memorial Day through July, the Padlock's hands live in tents, eat at a chuck wagon and sleep on bedrolls, just as their counterparts did a century ago. They rise at 3:30 a.m. for breakfast and often work until dusk, no matter the weather. Trips to town are infrequent, and a custom-made saddle, chaps and boots, silver inlaid spurs, bits and bridles may cost a cowboy an entire summer's wages.

A horseman crosses the mist-shrouded meadows of the Lucas Ranch near Jackson, Wyoming. At the turn of the century, these lands beneath the Teton Mountains were all prime cattle-grazing country. Today, Jackson is a resort town. Millions of tourists visit the area on their way to Grand Teton and Yellowstone national parks. Much of the valley's private land has been sold to developers. The Lucas family runs one of the last working ranches in Jackson.

W estcliffe, Colorado, lies in the Wet Mountain Valley beneath the Sangre de Cristo mountains. In the fall, a visitor strolling downtown can hear cattle bawling from the shipping pens a few blocks away. Tourism has changed many small towns, but Westcliffe retains its mixture of the beautiful and the eccentric. This building, eerily aglow in the moonlight, sits at the edge of town.

P atrons of the Cowboy Bar in Jackson, Wyoming, don't belly up to the bar. They straddle a saddle. But the saddles do more than impress the dudes and dudettes in this resort town. They're a matter of economics as well. Before installing the saddles, the bar went through three sets of stools. It has yet to replace a saddle. These classics were crafted by Colorado Saddlery in Denver.

*S*ilhouetted by a wind-whipped American flag, Merle G. Curtice, 84, pauses to enjoy the sun's warmth before breaking camp at Fort Casper, Wyoming. Curtice was part of the Wyoming Centennial Wagon Train's 260-mile, month-long journey across the state from Casper to Cody. Sixty-five covered wagons, six hundred horses and hundreds of travelers made the trek along the same path as the pioneers of more than a century ago.

P eople settled the high plains for many reasons, but most came during the homestead years in the late 1800s and early 1900s. Government land was free — if the owner stayed on the claim for five years and improved it. Homestead shacks like this one dotted Prairie County, Montana. But five years of bitter winters, rattlesnakes, drought, grasshoppers and the ever-present wind blowing a tune across the stove pipe proved the undoing of most homesteaders. Prairie County has fewer people today than it did in the 1930s.

N ot far from his family's original homestead, Quinn Haughians feeds ewes from his flock. Haughians' grandfather, Daniel, came to Montana by way of Ireland, Africa, Mexico and Oregon. Around the turn of the century, Daniel trailed sheep from Oregon to Montana, settling near the town of Terry. When Quinn was growing up, the family used a motorized tram to cross the Yellowstone River so he could catch the school bus. The tram, named "The Flying Susan," in honor of Quinn's grandmother, provided the only access to a paved road. "Sheep can live on almost nothing," says Quinn of his grandfather's legacy, "and a man can live on sheep."

There are places on the northern plains where you can find metal arrowheads beside long-abandoned train routes. The arrowheads are broken and bent after being shot into locomotive steel by Native American warriors trying to kill the iron horse. Whenever I see these power-line towers marching across the Wyoming plains near the town of Rock Springs, they look as alien to me as the trains did to the Indians.

*H*alfway through a month-long, four-hundred-mile float trip across Montana on the Yellowstone River, rafting guide Bob Wiltshire searches the shoreline for a camping spot. The dog's name is Stryder. Wiltshire lives in Livingston, Montana, and has spent much of his life on, in and beside the Yellowstone. He began this trip in mid-October and finished in late November at the Yellowstone's confluence with the Missouri River in North Dakota.

Although this church is in Montana, it could be anywhere on the grasslands of the Great Plains. Small, white buildings with their crosses against the sky are almost as much a part of this landscape as the earth itself. The spaces are great, the congregations small. Where there are no towns, the churches serve as community centers. Before becoming a church, the building may have been a one-room school. People have married and buried and danced and voted and prayed and learned to read in hundreds of buildings just like this.

A bull moose searches for underwater plants and marsh grasses worthy of a nibble as an early morning sun reflects in the Yellowstone River in Yellowstone National Park, Wyoming.

A setting sun drops behind a windmill in a west Texas sky tinted red by smoke from a rangefire. Sandhill cranes, traveling between feeding grounds and roosting areas, move across the landscape. The cranes winter in the warm climate along the Gulf of Mexico, then migrate as far north as Canada. The distinctive gurgling coo of the cranes and the squeaking of a windmill's blades create an unforgettable song of the plains.

ominated by 14,150-foot Mount Sneffels, the San Miguel Valley of south-western Colorado is one of the most beautiful places in the West. When the aspen and cotton-wood leaves yellow in autumn, the entire valley seems bathed in a golden light. Sneffels is a Norse word for "snowfield." Snow always seems to be present on the mountains in this range, retreating to the high places for only the briefest of interludes.

No matter how many times you've seen it, Arizona's Grand Canyon always startles. The land simply stops and drops into an immense void. Everything human ends. Far below, the Colorado River shimmers, a silent thread. Cloud shadows drift across vast plateaus, and sunlight plays across a maze of rock walls. This view is taken from the North Rim.

*L*ittle Chief and Citadel peaks catch the first light of daybreak as they tower above St. Mary's Lake in Glacier-Waterton National Peace Park. The park, on the border of Montana and British Columbia, was created in 1932 as an act of good will between the United States and Canada. Covering 2,000 square miles, the park is part of an international network of Biosphere Reserves, providing, according to the dedicatory plaque, "a standard against which can be measured the effects of man's impact on his environment."

A bright winter moon glides across a stormy sky above the plains along U.S. 56 near Clayton, New Mexico. This nocturnal vista symbolizes the West — all that land and sky, all that space and nothing in it. The emptiness, wind and silence seem over-whelming, broken only by an occasional ranch house, a few cattle or horses and maybe a human or two.

*A*ll the streets in Otis, Colorado, end in prairie or cropland. On a winter night, the pool hall and Hagler's General Store next door offer the only signs of life. The 70-year-old pool hall also serves the community as a cafe, video arcade and gathering spot. "People seem to think a pool hall is just for men. That's not true here," says Mardel White, the hall's owner. "As many women come here as men. Even cops and preachers drop by. Everybody's welcome. I cherish every customer."

*S*teamboat Springs, Colorado, may be as famous for its hot springs as its skiing. An unpaved dirt road north of town helps keep Strawberry Hot Springs secluded. Although a sign at the hot springs entrance advises against nudity, this bather found the invigorating pools deserted enough for a skinny dip in the middle of a winter day.

G listening with snow, the summits of Colorado's Collegiate Peaks part the clouds on a winter day. The Collegiates, photographed here from the window of a passing jet, are part of the Sawatch Range, which stretches 90 miles from the Eagle River in the north to Poncha Pass in the south. The range contains fifteen peaks of more than 14,000 feet in elevation.

*N*early a million of Yellowstone National Park's 2.5 million acres burned during the fires of 1988. All summer long, a red sun cast an eerie pink light through the park. Smoke billowed thousands of feet into the air. This forested hillside and countless others like it were devoured. Hellish winds cast embers miles ahead of the flames. But in the blackened aftermath there was beauty to be found. Beneath the snow was a latent promise of spring and a new beginning for the century-old park.

*K*evin Wahlert's family has ranched on Derby Mesa since 1892. The closest town is Burns, Colorado, reached by a 20-mile drive on a steep, switchbacked dirt and gravel road barely wide enough for one car. Burns consists of a church, gas station and store. Wahlert wouldn't have it any other way. Burns is enough civilization for him. He'd rather be out riding beneath a full moon in big country, moving cattle on a night so cold the horses' hooves squeak out sweet music in the snow.

All summer long, the VanValkenburg family summers its cattle in the high mountain meadows of North Park, Colorado. In late October, with the season's first snow on the ground and storm clouds swirling around Rabbit Ears Peak, it's time to bring the cattle down toward the home ranch, where they'll winter. Autumn is the ranchers' time of harvest, when the fatted calf is weaned, sold and shipped and a year's labor marked up to profit or loss.

Easy does it as Kevin Wahlert and Larry Lynch gentle a colt on the century-old Albertson Ranch on Colorado's Derby Mesa. After a day of work, the colt is the last of the evening's chores, its bucking and snorting and kicking more amusement than a threat to the two men. Named Milkface, the colt is a Christmas present for Wahlert's wife, Jelaine.

Almost anything can grow in the fertile soil of Colorado's San Luis Valley. This weird tree, of course, did not. The recycled restaurant decoration was planted by Manuel Montano, who owns "The Junque Factory," near Center. "I'll buy, sell or trade almost anything," he says.

*T*his barn along U.S. 89 near Emigrant, Montana, once served as a rest station for early tourists on their way to Yellowstone National Park. When the park was established in 1872, most visitors traveled by stagecoach or other horse-powered means. At places like this, they spent the night, repaired wagons, bought supplies and rested their mounts before the next leg of the journey.

H igh on the flanks of Mount Everts in Yellowstone National Park, bighorn sheep rams brave a driving December snowstorm. Rams usually battle each other over ewes during the late fall breeding season, but this group stuck together, formed a single-file line and made its way to lower country in search of shelter and easier grazing.

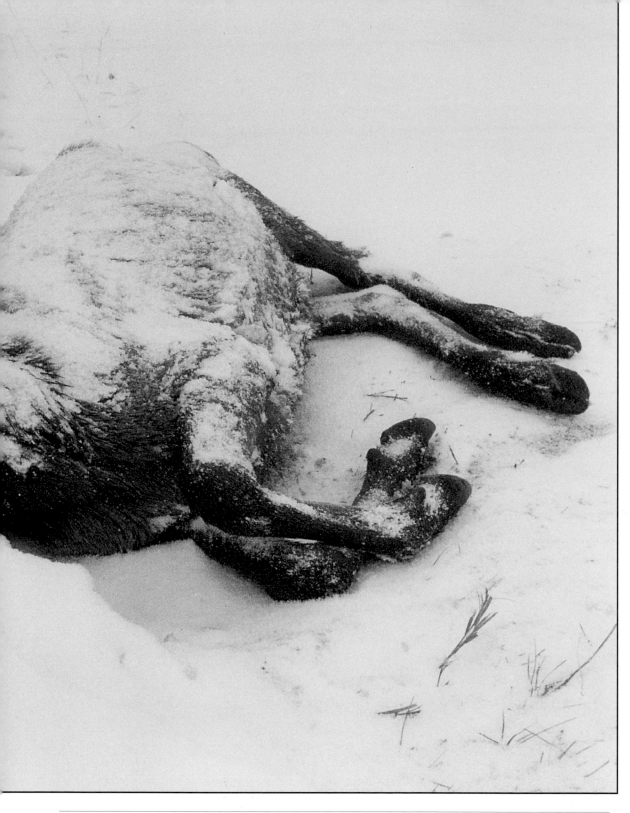

A starving cow elk lies in the snow, unable to get up in the Lamar Valley of Yellowstone National Park. The fires that burned nearly half of Yellowstone during the summer of 1988 blackened much of the elk's winter ranges. Thousands of elk starved to death. Despite public outcry to feed the herds, Yellowstone officials held firm in the park's policy of non-interference. The elk population was unnaturally high, they said. Starvation would reduce their numbers. But the process was painful to watch.

Dean Krakel, 41, has been a photographer with Denver's Rocky Mountain News since 1987. A native of Wyoming, he has written two books. "Season of the Elk" chronicles the seasonal migration of elk herds through the rugged wilderness areas of northwestern Wyoming. "Downriver — A Yellowstone Journey" follows the 671-mile course of the Yellowstone River. Krakel lives in Conifer, Colo., with his wife, Alisa, and three sons.